# DOG ANTIQUES AND COLLECTIBLES

Patricia Robak

Schiffer Publishing Ltd

4880 Lower Valley Road, Atglen, PA 19310 USA

# DEDICATION

To the spirit and soul of my Chip (1984-1996)

Title page photo:
Tinted sepia postcard, "Three Beauties," Raphael Tuck & Sons, England, ca. 1915. 5.5" h. x 3.5" w. $7-10.

Published by Schiffer Publishing Ltd.
4880 Lower Valley Road
Atglen, PA 19310
Phone: (610) 593-1777; Fax: (610) 593-2002
E-mail: Schifferbk@aol.com
Please visit our web site catalog at **www.schifferbooks.com**

This book may be purchased from the publisher.
Include $3.95 for shipping.
Please try your bookstore first.
We are interested in hearing from authors
with book ideas on related subjects.
You may write for a free catalog.

In Europe, Schiffer books are distributed by
Bushwood Books
6 Marksbury Rd.
Kew Gardens
Surrey TW9 4JF England
Phone: 44 (0)181 392-8585; Fax: 44 (0)181 392-9876
E-mail: Bushwd@aol.com

# CONTENTS

(Top) Victorian chromolithograph calling card with head of St. Bernard, ca. 1870-90. 1.75" h. x 3.5" w. (Bottom) Trade card with puppies in basket, ca. 1870-90. 2.25" h. x 4.25" w. Calling card, $5-7. Trade card, $6-8.

# ACKNOWLEDGMENTS

In preparing this book, I would like to extend special thanks to Stephen D. Compton, Hamilton, Ohio; Betty Fitzgerald, Rhode Island Collections Librarian, Providence (Rhode Island) Public Library; Thomas Gaffney, Special Collections Librarian, Portland Room, Portland (Maine) Public Library; Barbara Kolk, American Kennel Club Library, New York City, New York; and Gregory H. Laing, Special Collections Librarian, Haverhill (Massachusetts) Public Library.

Handmade orange ribbon photograph holder with blue crocheted circles, with sepia cabinet card photograph of dog and toddler, ca. 1890-1910. 14.5" h. x 5.5" w. $50-65.

# INTRODUCTION

Let's admit it—if you love dogs, you want them around you all the time. In addition to the real thing, the beloved, inspiring images of their faces and forms are something we dog lovers never tire of admiring. Maybe that's why the image of the dog on all sorts of objects—utilitarian, decorative, or both—has been a part of the material cultures of several civilizations for centuries. Many books on the history of the dog and its close relationship with humans have pictured the Egyptian dog god Anubis, the Mastiffs of the Assyrians, and the mythological hounds of Diana, Roman goddess of hunting. Antique Chinese figures of temple dogs, Japanese prints of playful puppies, and Inuit carvings of sled dogs are familiar reminders of the dog's prominence in our collective memory.

It's difficult to discuss the scope of the dog's involvement with humankind without lapsing into clichés—"Faithful Companion," "Man's Best Friend," "All of the virtues, none of the vices," "The more I see of [fill in the blank], the more I like my dog." Time-worn as they are, these phrases are still meaningful, and their visual counterparts remain eminently popular: the watchful sheepdog next to the dozing shepherd, the grieving hound at his master's grave, the Newfoundland patrolling the shoreline, the Collie gazing intelligently at a toddler who asks, "Can't you talk?"

As the examples above indicate, anthropomorphism—imbuing an animal with human characteristics—is very much in evidence in the world of dog antiques. It can be charming, whimsical, entertaining, or cloying, depending on your personal point of view. A favorite device of the often-melodramatic Victorians, the intent of anthropomorphism became mordantly effective when it was used in political cartoons or wartime propaganda.

The images of dogs in western popular culture from the early nineteenth century through 1950 are those which represent the primary scope of this book. Other works, such as William Secord's superb *Dog Painting, 1840-1940: A Social History of the Dog in Art* and Robert Rosenblum's erudite *The Dog in Art From Rococo to Post-Modernism*, have addressed the subject of dogs in art in an extensive and scholarly fashion. And additional books are available on more specialized areas, such as the canine image in old advertisements (*The Dog Made Me Buy It!*, by Alice L. Muncaster and Ellen Sawyer), Staffordshire spaniel figures (*Staffordshire Spaniels*, by Adele Kenny), collecting a specific breed (*A Treasury of Scottie Dog Collectibles*, by Candace Sten Davis and Patricia Baugh), and famous established collections (*A Dog Lover's Collection* by Achille Alessandro Conti and Ptolemy Tompkins). These books, and more, are listed in the Bibliography found at the end of this book.

Chromolithograph trade card in monotone, "Can't You Talk," child and Collie, advertising Frarey's Albany Shoes, ca. 1870-90. One of the most enduring, and endearing, dog images of Victorian popular culture, the "Can't You Talk" scene shows up frequently on prints, ceramics, statuary, and textiles. 2.75" h. x 4.25" w. $6-8.

The goal of this book, in contrast, is to explore an eclectic and mid-range level of dog antiques and pre-1950 collectible items which are interesting, accessible, and affordable. The book is primarily organized based on the type of material used, so some items—figures and boxes, for example—may appear in more than one chapter. Not included here are collectible porcelains (Royal Doulton, Hutschenreuther, Rosenthal, and the like), Mortens figures, stuffed toys, blatant caricature items, or items made after 1950. Neither grandiose nor silly, the items photographed and identified in this book are pretty much the artifacts of a rising middle class—one leisured enough to maintain pet animals for pleasure and for sport, and affluent enough to commission and purchase items commemorating them. Sentimental and affectionate toward their dogs, these people had their dogs' portraits done, engraved their names on elegant collars, included them in family photographs, and bought books about them for children and adults alike. The canine image on everything from candy boxes to cabinetry made it clear that the dog—then, as now— was happily embraced in the everyday lives of humans.

## A NOTE ON VALUES

It is important to remember than a value range can only be a rough estimate of an item's worth. The values in this book are retail, for items in good condition unless otherwise noted, and were set in late 1998 in non-metropolitan New England. They should not be used to set pricing, since many variables need to be considered in one's own situation, such as geographic region, current supply and demand, specific auction and show action, item condition, and, in the particular case of dog-related objects, breed popularity, breed rarity in antiques, and sentiment.

Pair of studio photographs of boy in winter clothes with black Cocker Spaniel, ca. 1900-1915. Each 5.5" h. x 4" w. $45-65/pair.

Iron doorstop of standing German Shepherd Dog, trestle base, silver finish, marked "Davison," ca. 1920-40. 12" h. x 13" w. $150-200.

# DOG BREEDS: TRENDS THROUGH TIME

As a dog antiques dealer who always wishes she had something in stock for everyone, my heart sinks a little when I am asked, "Do you have any Shiba Inu things?" or even "Got any Chocolate Lab antiques?" In the case of the newly-popular Shiba Inu, a Japanese breed, as well as the more familiar Labrador, these breeds did not catch the public's fancy until after 1950 or so, and therefore their images do not frequently show up on antiques or older collectibles.

Lithograph illustration of various dog breeds, source unknown, France, ca. 1915-30. 11.5" h. x 15.5" w. $50-65.

Engraving of six dog breeds, Greyhound, Spaniel, Harrier, Foxhound, Pointer, Terrier. J. Neagle, 1825. 10" h. x 8" w. $100-150.

Some currently popular breeds, however, such as the Golden Retriever, Bernese Mountain Dog, and Rottweiler, for instance, are rare but possible finds on antiques . . . if you are flexible enough to accept a close resemblance, at least! I have had a Swiss postcard, ca. 1910, picturing what I think is a Bernese, a Victorian trade card with what certainly looks like a Golden carrying lilies in its mouth, and an unusual carte de visite photograph from Maine, ca. 1880, of a dog which truly resembles a Rottweiler. You just never know—and this accounts, of course, for a lot of the fun, challenge, and adventure of collecting dog antiques!

Looking backwards in time, it's easy to identify certain breeds with certain decades. The Poodle craze of the 1950s overlapped the great popularity of the German Shepherd Dog (whose cinematic fame actually started in the 1920s) as well as that of the Collie, whose good looks and noble deeds made great movies and television. Before that, during the 1930s and 1940s, Cocker Spaniels and Scottish Terriers (the latter greatly popularized by Franklin Delano Roosevelt's Scottie, Fala) showed up on everything from children's books to cocktail napkins. Even earlier, in the 1920s and 1930s, a frequent motif in the Art Déco style was the elegant Russian Wolfhound, or Borzoi, along with an often-stylized version of the Wire-haired Fox Terrier.

With all the recent bad press about the dog now known as the pit bull, it might surprise many readers to learn that this sturdy breed, variously known as the American Staffordshire Terrier, Staffordshire Bull Terrier, or American Pit Bull Terrier, was America's family dog in the early years of the twentieth century. There are plenty of old sepia photographic postcards that picture this dog lolling among the family on a farmhouse porch, posing nicely with starched and beribboned children, or grinning from the front seat of a new Model T. As a matter of fact, the illustrator Wallace Robinson chose this breed as the canine symbol of the United States during World War I.

At the turn of the nineteenth century into the twentieth, the Smooth-coated Fox Terrier (from which the Jack Russell strain was bred in the late nineteenth century), the English Bulldog, and the sporting setters and pointers were the breeds most commonly seen on mass-produced objects. A few decades earlier, during the 1870s, the number of field trials and dog shows began rising significantly in both Britain and America. As a result, interest in breed standards and the introduction of new breeds of dogs was steadily growing, as was the dedication of many to animal humane society efforts. In Great Britain, Queen Victoria, Prince Albert, and their family members were all great dog lovers, and their prominence, influence, and patronage of animal artists brought the pleasures of dog ownership into the public eye, both at home and abroad.

Prior to the late nineteenth century, dogs were either the working and/or sporting types—herding livestock on family farms, fetching game for hunters, running around in circular cages to work turnspits, and often serving as the object of sport themselves, in the case of early bull-baiting

dogs—or they were the pampered pets of the upper and middle classes. From this latter group, we see images of spunky little terriers at play with children, or delicate Whippets and winsome spaniels on fine ceramics. Especially in the sentimental Victorian era, the pairing of small children (vulnerability and innocence) with large dogs (safety and trustworthiness) was frequently depicted, and it is from this time period that we see the familiar pictorial variations of the Mastiff guarding a cradle or the Newfoundland rescuing a child from drowning.

Often, however, we are struck by the difference in the way a certain breed looks now, compared to its appearance more than a hundred years ago. For instance, the dog called a "Retriever" in the Richard Ansdell lithograph on page 30 looks much more like today's black Newfoundland than any sort of present-day retriever breed. And the Landseer Newfoundland pictured in the painting on page 12 (so-named because the famous artist Sir Edwin Landseer popularized the black and white color variation in the mid-nineteenth century) appears to have a somewhat more lightweight appearance, with a different muzzle shape, than the conformation of today's Newfoundland. In fact, the dog from the painting actually resembles the dog identified as a St. Bernard in the 1880 illustration of six dog breeds shown on this page. Moreover, the Cocker Spaniel in this same illustration has the look of a slightly fluffy Beagle!

It is always fascinating to look at representations of breeds in the past, especially when they are identified. Besides reading breed histories, studying these old images is a good way to learn about your favorite breed's "ancestors," especially if you are interested in building an historically-oriented collection. Several books listed in the Bibliography combine illustrations with informative text and can be very helpful resources for studying the background and development of dog breeds through history.

Chromolithograph illustration of six dog breeds, Fox Hound, Pointer, Blood Hound, St. Bernard, King Charles Spaniel, Cocker Spaniel, from *Johnson's Household Book of Nature*, ca. 1880. 6" h. x 8" w. $50-60.

# Chapter 1
# PAINTINGS, DRAWINGS, AND PRINTS

## PAINTINGS AND DRAWINGS

Oil on board painting of setter with bird, signed J. Langlois (English), late nineteenth century. 12" h. x 14" w. *Courtesy of Weston H. Palmer.* $1200-1400.

Oil on board painting of two terriers,
signed J. Langlois (English), late
nineteenth century. 12" h. x 14" w.
*Courtesy of Weston H. Palmer.*
$1200-1400.

Oil on canvas painting of Landseer
Newfoundland at shore, signed
Elshemus, late nineteenth century. 8.5"
h. x 11" w. $650-750.

Oil on canvas painting of three young dogs in barn, signed Nellie C. Cooper, date illegible, probably early twentieth century. 7.5" h. x 9.25" w. $400-475.

Primitive oil on canvas painting of head of Pointer against landscape, unsigned, late nineteenth century. 24" h. x 19" w. $475-575.

Primitive oil on canvas over board, Pointer staring at bird, unsigned, second half nineteenth century. 15" h. x 13" w. $450-500.

Hand-painted album card, watercolor on card stock, Pointer staring at bird, unsigned, second half nineteenth century. 4" h. x 2.5" w. $35-50.

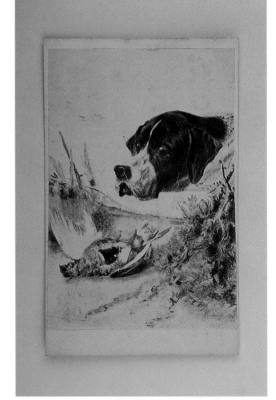

Primitive oil on canvas, setter sitting in forest glade, unsigned, late nineteenth century. 29" h. x 21" w. $650-700.

Oil on canvas over board painting of recumbent English Bulldog, signed Morgan Dennis (American, 1892-1960). This painting, after the original by Frederic Stanley, depicts the trademark dog of the J.P. Hanley Brewery of Providence, Rhode Island; see the Hanley beer tray on page 69. Ca. 1940-50. 21.5" h. x 29.5" w. $1800-2000.

Watercolor on paper portrait of Long-haired Dachshund, identified as Redledge Moritz from pedigree attached to back of frame, signed Nichols, ca. 1935. 14.5" h. x 10.5" w. $350-400.

Pastel on paper portrait of French Bulldog, signed H. Hyman, ca. 1915-30. 21.5" h. x 17.5" w. $275-325.

Pastel on paper portrait of Irish Setter, signed Helen Wilson Sherman '48 [1948]. 25.25" h. x 20.25" w. $225-275.

Charcoal and pastel on paper studies of Boxer, signed H. C. Wolcott, ca. 1930-50. 16.75" h. x 22" w. $225-275.

Charcoal and pastel on paper drawing of King Charles Spaniel and Border Terrier in winter scene, initialed "I.J.C 1880." 10.25" h. x 15" w. This image portrays Victorian social class consciousness, symbolized by dogs. $225-275.

Charcoal and pastel on paper head of English Setter, signed Gladys Emerson Cook (American, 1899-1977), ca. 1930-50. 11.75" h. x 16" w. $250-300.

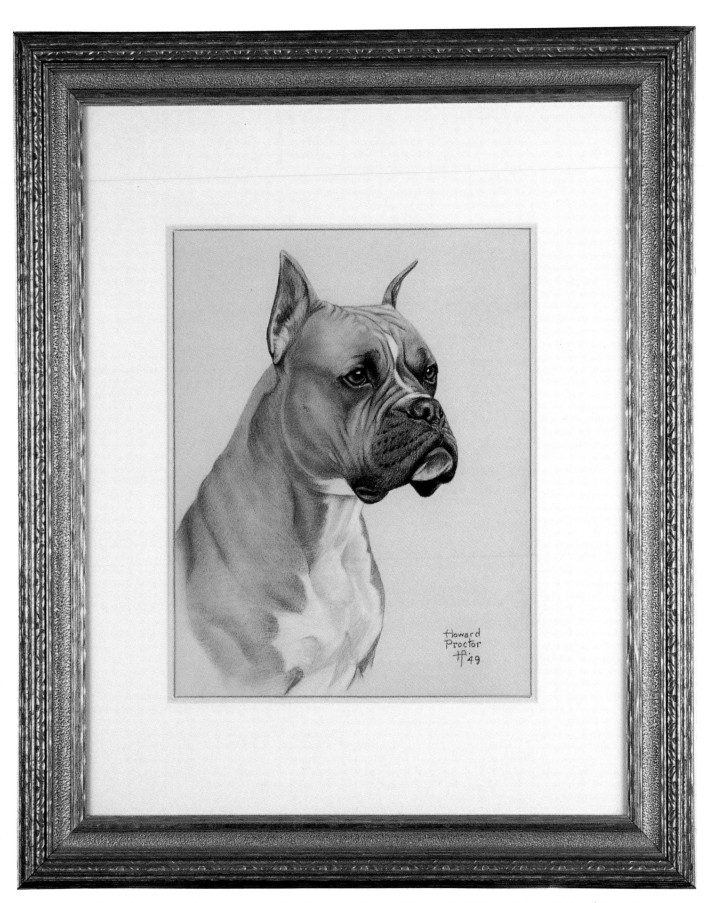

Pencil, pastel, and watercolor on paper portrait of Boxer, signed Howard Proctor '49 [1949.] 23.5" h. x 19.25" w.  $350-450.

Charcoal and pastel on paper head of St. Bernard, unsigned, late nineteenth-early twentieth century. 13.5" h. x 10.5" w. A very popular canine image of the era, this three-quarters view of the head of a trusty St. Bernard was a favorite of amateur artists and a familiar sight today to collectors of dog antiques. $325-375.

Pencil on paper drawing of hunting dogs and grouse, unsigned, second half nineteenth century. 19" h. x 15" w. $200-250.

Pencil on paper sketches of dog, signed S. Kitchen, entitled "Spot - Aug - 23 - 1928." 9" h. x 11.5" w. $40-50.

Pen and ink drawing on paper, unsigned, caricature of Theodore J. Roosevelt with English Bulldog resembling him, entitled "Who's Coming?" Ca. 1905. 7.5" h. x 11.25" w. $75-100.

Pen and ink on paper drawing of three dogs, entitled "For Betty From Edward," signed Spencer, ca. 1930-50. 4.5" h. x 7.5" w. $65-85.

Hand-colored lithograph, "Beagles," Henry Alken, published by T. McLean, London, 1820. 6" h. x 8.5" w. $250-325.

Hand-colored engraving, "All A-Blowin'!" [blooming], flower-selling girl with spaniel, published by S. & J. Fuller, London, 1812. 5.25" h. x 5.25" w. $200-250.

Hand-colored lithograph, "The Fox-Hunter," Foxhounds, James S. Baillie, New York City, ca. 1838-55. 9" h. x 13" w. $175-225.

Hand-colored lithograph, "Partridge Shooting. Plate 2," Pointer, setter, and black and tan hound, Henry Alken, published by S. & J. Fuller, London, 1835. 8.5" x 11" w. $300-350.

Hand-colored lithograph, "My Little Playfellow," boy with spaniel, James S. Baillie, New York City, ca. 1838-55. 16.5" h. x 12.5" w. $175-225.

Black and white lithograph, "Good Morning! Little Favorite," terrier and baby, Currier & Ives, New York City, ca. 1857-1872. 12.25" h. x 9" w. $175-225.

Black and white lithograph, "Retriever and Pheasant," after original by Richard Ansdell (English, 1815-1885), mid-nineteenth century. 13.75" x 11.25" w. This particular retrieving dog resembles today's black Newfoundland. $250-300.

AMERICAN FIELD SPORTS.

Hand-colored lithograph, "American Field Sports No. 2," L.M. Delavan, New York City, ca. 1868. Spaniel and Pointer. 19" h. x 24.5" w. $375-475.

Chromolithograph, Landseer New-foundland, Prince Charles Spaniel, and cat in Victorian parlor setting, ca. 1883. 13" h. x 15" w. $75-85.

31

Chromolithograph print, "Doggie's Lesson," Pug, after original by M. Goodman, ca. 1895. 16" h. x 8" w. $80-95.

Chromolithograph print, "Good News," Greyhound, published by P.O. Vickery, Augusta, Maine, ca. 1887. 19.5" h. x 14" w. $80-95.

Chromolithograph print, "I'll Hold Him," published by P.O. Vickery, Augusta, Maine, 1889. 23" h. x 14" w. $80-95.

 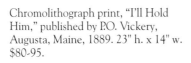

Chromolithograph print with self-folding frame, "Family Cares," girl with kitten and puppy, Art Supplement to The Boston Globe, 1905. 11.75" h. x 9.5" w. $20-30.

Sepia etching, "Out of the Hunt," signed by Frank Paton (English, 1858-1909), published by Leggett Bros., London, 1892. 8.25" h. x 10.25" w. $800-1000.

Chromolithograph illustration, "Skye Terriers. 'Sam', the Property of Mr. Mark Gretton. 'Perkie', the Property of Mr. James Locke," from *The Illustrated Book of the Dog*, London, Cassell, 1879-81. 13" h. x 15" w. $175-225.

Chromolithograph illustration, "St. Bernard. 'Abbess'," from *The Illustrated Book of the Dog*, London, Cassell, 1879-81. 13" h. x 15" w. $175-225.

Black and white print of two Dandie Dinmont Terriers, after original by Arthur Wardle (English, 1864-1949), ca. 1915. 13.5" h. x 17.25" w. $225-275.

Color print, "Playing Days, Welsh Springer Puppies," after original by Maud Earl (English, 1864-1943), published by the Berlin Photographic Company, Berlin and London, 1905. 8.25" h. x 14" w. $275-350.

Monotone print, "Protection," four Great Danes, published by E.A. Wright Bank Note Company, Philadelphia, ca. 1910. 5.5" h. x 7.5" w. $65-85.

Etching of head of German Shepherd Dog, signed David Gee, ca. 1930-50. 5" h. x 5" w. $100-150.

Black and white photogravure print, "A Happy Dog," Keeshond, after original by H. Bever, published by Gebbie & Husson Co., Ltd., ca. 1895. 11" h. x 8.5" w. $150-200.

Sepia photogravure print, "The Fox Hounds of Vendée," after original by Charles Oliver De Penne, published by Gebbie & Husson Co., Ltd., ca. 1895. 14" h. x 10.25" w. $150-200.

Black transfer-printed cup and saucer, hunting dog motif, pink lustre trim, unmarked, probably England, ca. 1820-40. Saucer: 5.5" diam.; cup: 2.5" h. x 3.5" diam. $75-100/set.

Rectangular white ironstone dish, bas-relief motif of Diana, Roman goddess of hunting, and her hounds, ca. 1850. 4.25" h. x 5.5" w. $50-65.

Brown transfer-printed plate, "Baronial Halls" pattern by T. J. & J. Mayer, Staffordshire, England, ca. 1843-55. 7" diam.

Detail, showing hunting dogs.

Brown transfer-printed cup and saucer, unmarked but probably "Veranda" pattern by Ralph Hall & Co., Staffordshire, England, ca. 1841-49. Saucer: 6" diam.; cup: 2.5" h. x 4.5" diam. $65-85/set.

Detail of top left photo, showing boy and Greyhound.

Brown transfer-printed plate with raised vine border, "Partridge Shooting," unmarked but probably England, ca. 1860-80. 7.5" diam. $85-125.

Detail of bottom left photo, showing English Setter in plate border.

Brown transfer-printed plate, "Melton" pattern by Wedgwood & Co., Staffordshire, England, registry mark for 1883. 9.5" diam. $40-50. This firm of Wedgwood & Co., formerly Podmore, Walker & Co., is not to be confused with "the" Wedgwood—Josiah Wedgwood & Sons. For clarification, see Geoffrey Godden's *Encyclopaedia of British Pottery and Porcelain Marks*, listed in the bibliography on page 157.

Brown transfer-printed and tan lustre plate, saucer, and cup, "Sporting Scenes" pattern by J.F. Wileman, Staffordshire, England, ca. 1870-90. Plate: 7.25" diam.; saucer: 6" diam.; cup: 2.5" h. x 3.5" diam. Plate: $50-65. Cup and saucer: $75-95.

Child-sized red transfer teapot and lid, same pattern as preceding photo, Staffordshire, England, ca. 1891. 5.25" h. $85-100.

Child-sized blue transfer-printed plate, cup, and saucer, girl on stoop with terrier and cats. Staffordshire, England, registry mark for 1888. Plate: 5.25" diam.; saucer: 4.5" diam.; cup: 2" h. x 2.5" diam. Plate: $40-50. Cup and saucer: $65-85.

Child-sized blue transfer-printed plate, cup, and saucer, girl with large dog. Staffordshire, England, registry mark for 1887. Plate: 6.75" diam.; cup: 2.5" h. x 3" diam.; saucer, 5.25" diam. Plate: $40-50. Cup and saucer: $65-85.

Transfer-printed and hand-painted plate, scene of child with dog and cat embellished with floral sprays, Pinder, Bourne & Co., Staffordshire, England, ca. 1880. 9.25" diam. $85-100.

Shaded brown ceramic cider or ale pitcher, hound's head motif, with three matching mugs (out of a probable set of six or more) with different dogs' heads, unmarked but U.S., ca. 1900-15. Pitcher: 13" h. Each mug: 4.25" h. Pitcher: $100-150. Each mug: $35-45.

Tip-proof child's feeding dish, child and puppies motif, marked "Royal Baby-Plate / Pat. February 7, 1905." 8.5" diam. $75-95.

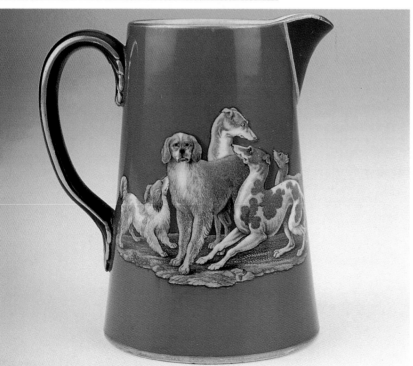

Left and above:
Turquoise ceramic jug with black and gold handle and spout, motif of dogs of various breeds on both sides of jug, unmarked but probably England, second half nineteenth century. 5" h. $200-250.

Hand-painted porcelain plate, English Setter in field, signed B. Aubin, Limoges, France, late nineteenth-early twentieth century. 9.5" diam. This plate (along with the others shown here and on page 48, top) was designed to be hung on a wall or displayed on a stand as a decorative object. $175-225.

Calendar plate for 1908, hound's head in center, The National China Co., East Liverpool, Ohio, ca. 1907. 9" diam. $75-95.

Pair of decorative plates, hunting dogs, Germany, ca. 1900-1915. Each 8" diam. $50-65 each.

Souvenir plate, humorous dogs motif, Trenle China Co., East Liverpool, Ohio, ca. 1910-20. 7.25" diam. $40-50.

American china plate, dog's head, unmarked, ca. 1910. 8" diam. $30-40.

Transfer-printed and hand-painted ceramic pot lid, scene of terriers causing trouble, probably England, second half nineteenth century. Twentieth-century round frame. Pot lid only: 4" diam. $250-275.

Yellowware covered box with recumbent Greyhound or Whippet on lid, unmarked, second half nineteenth century. 5.5" h. x 6.5" w. x 4" d. *Courtesy of Weston H. Palmer.* $375-450.

Painted earthenware matchsafe, recumbent terrier on lid, probably Germany, late nineteenth century. 4" h. x 7" w. x 3.5" d. *Courtesy of John Calderwood Weld.* $250-300.

Brown ceramic ashtray, central raised head of German Shepherd Dog in Seeing-Eye harness, bordered with the alphabet in Braille. Unmarked but probably U.S., ca. 1930-50. $35-45.

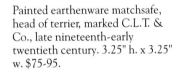

Painted earthenware matchsafe, head of terrier, marked C.L.T. & Co., late nineteenth-early twentieth century. 3.25" h. x 3.25" w. $75-95.

Oval china matchsafe with recumbent Greyhound or Whippet on lid, late nineteenth century. 3.5" h. x 2" w. $65-85.

Glazed pottery dog dish, unmarked, ca. 1930-50. 6" diam. $45-65.

Painted earthenware smoking accessory holder, retriever-type dog with three baskets, late nineteenth century. Some repaint. 8" h. x 9" w. $125-150.

Pressed glass mug with dog motif, late nineteenth century. 3.5" h. $50-75.

Pressed glass mug with dog motif, late nineteenth century. 2.75" h. $50-75.

Opaque white glass disk with hand-painted dog's head, ca. 1880-1910. 8" diam. $60-85.

Pair of ruby and frosted glass vases, dog and birds motif, Central Europe, ca. 1890. Each 9" h. $195-225/pair.

Opaque white glass disk with hand-painted dog's head, painted on back: "Ella Maple St. 1880-1890." 12.5" diam. $85-100.

Black glass French Bulldog advertising figure, one eye missing, "Austin's Dog Bread" painted on back, "I Eat It" painted on chest, ca. 1910-30. 2.5" h. x 2.5" w. $75-100.

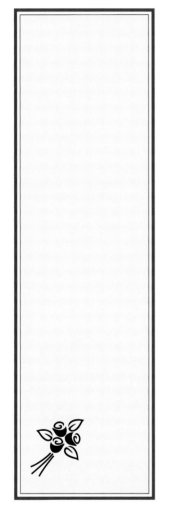

Glass pitcher, motif of dogs on leashes, ca. 1930-45. 8.5" h. $45-65.

Glass ashtray, Wire-haired Fox Terrier with ball, ca. 1930-50. 2.5" h. x 3.25" w. $20-30.

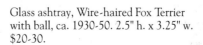

# Chapter 3
# METAL

## FIGURES

White metal recumbent dog figure, worn pewter-like finish, ca. 1890-1915. 2" h. x 6" w. $80-100.

White metal standing Pointer figure, bronze finish, ca. 1920-40. 3.25" h. x 4.75" w. $45-65.

White metal standing Sealyham Terrier figure, copper finish, ca. 1920-40. 2.5" h. x 4" w. $45-65.

White metal standing English Bulldog figure, copper finish, ca. 1930-50. 2.5" h. x 4.25" w. $40-50.

White metal standing terrier figure, bright bronze finish, ca. 1930-50. 4" h. x 4.5" w. $45-60.

White metal recumbent Greyhound figure, worn brass finish, ca. 1930-50. 3" h. x 6" w. $50-65.

MARCH

| Su | Mo | Tu | We | Th | Fr | Sa |
|---|---|---|---|---|---|---|
| 1 | 2 | 3 | 4 | 5 | 6 | 7 |
| 8 | 9 | 10 | 11 | 12 | 13 | 14 |
| 15 | 16 | 17 | 18 | 19 | 20 | 21 |
| 22 | 23 | 24 | 25 | 26 | 27 | 28 |
| 29 | 30 | 31 | | | | |

Figural white metal desk calendar, standing spaniel figure, brass finish, souvenir of Luray Caverns, Virginia, ca. 1930-50. 3.5" h. x 6" w. $65-85.

White metal standing spaniel figure, copper finish, ca. 1930-50. 2.25" h. x 3" w. $30-45.

White metal standing Scottish Terrier figure, black finish, ca. 1930-50. 1.5" h. x 2" w. $20-30.

White metal hairpin box with standing terrier figure, worn silver finish, ca. 1880-1910. 2.5" h. x 3.25" w. $85-125.

White metal sitting Boxer puppy figure, bronze finish, ca. 1930-50. 1.5" h. x 1.75" w. $30-45.

Primitive lead figure of sitting dog, extremely worn finish, late nineteenth century. 2.5" h. x 1.75" w. $30-45.

Iron standing Scottish terrier figural paperweight, marked "Hamilton Foundry / Quality Castings," ca. 1945-50. 2.25" h. x 3.5" w. This item was given out to those who toured the Hamilton, Ohio foundry which manufactured it. $65-85.

Small bronze standing Scottish Terrier sculpture, signed P. Dreux, early twentieth century. 2" h. x 2.5" w. $200-300.

One of a pair of iron German Shepherd Dog bookends, sitting dog in outdoor scene, bronze finish, ca. 1920-40. 5.75" h. x 4.5" w. $95-125/pair.

Single iron bookend, German Shepherd Dog at gate, bronze finish, ca. 1920-40. 6" h. x 5.25" w. $65-85.

Pair of white metal sitting German Shepherd Dog bookends, bronze finish, ca. 1930-50. 7" h. x 5" w. $75-95/pair.

Metal, wall-mounted outdoor bell surmounted by standing spaniel figure, marked "B.N.C 11 U.S.A." Ca. 1950. 15" h. x 7" w. Bell: 6.5" diam. $125-150.

Iron doorstop, Scottish Terrier balancing circle with name RUDY, ca. 1930-50. 13" h. x 6" w. $150-175.

Primitive iron Dachshund bootscraper, old green paint, ca. 1920-40. 6.5" h. x 11" w. $75-100.

 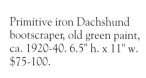

Iron ornamental tray, central motif of fighting dogs, original paint, second half nineteenth century. 7" h. x 13" w. $150-195.

Iron sitting Scottish Terrier lamp, electric, ca. 1940-50, shown here with new shade. 13.5" h. x 5.75" w. $75-95.

Dog faces in bas-relief. (Left) Bronze dish, ca. 1890-1915. 5.75" diam. $75-95. (Right) Iron wall plaque, original paint all but worn off, ca. 1880-1910. 5" diam. $75-95.

Brass ashtray, two setters in field, Virginia Metalcrafters, ca. 1950. 3.25" h. x 4.5" w. $30-45.

Brass ashtray, head of Pointer, ca. 1950. 5" diam. $30-45.

Pair of small bronze trays, Pointers, ca. 1930-50. Each 3" h. x 4.25" w. $45-65 each.

Hammered aluminum ashtray with dog and ball motif at rim, ca. 1930-50. 6" diam. $40-50.

Brass Art Déco terrier bottle opener, ca. 1930-40. 5" h. $60-70.

Silverplated mug, dog figure surmounting handle, Meriden (Connecticut), ca. 1880-1898. 5" h. $90-125.

Detail of dog figure on the mug.

Silverplated napkin ring with leaping dog motif, unmarked, ca. 1885. .75" h. x 1.5" diam. $65-85.

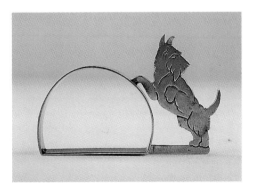

Silvertoned metal napkin ring with Scottish Terrier motif, ca. 1930-1940. 1.75" h. x 2.75" w. $35-45.

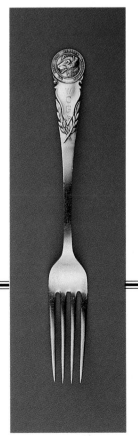

Silverplated dinner fork, "The Wire Fox Terrier Association," head of Wire-haired Fox Terrier, England, early twentieth century. 7" long. $60-75.

Brass toasting fork with begging dog figure on handle, England, ca. 1930-50. 19" long. $45-65.

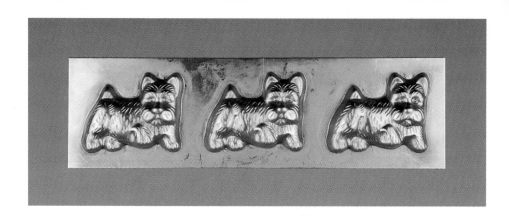

Metal candy mold, three Scottish Terriers, ca. 1930-50. 2.5" h. x 9" w. $50-75.

Tin candy mold, head of Pointer, early twentieth century. 2.25" h. x 4" w. $75-95.

Dog-shaped tin cookie cutter, ca. 1930-50. 2.5" h. x 3" w. $8-10.

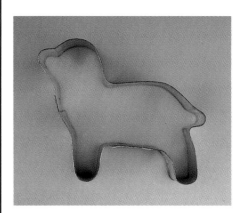

Dog-shaped tin cookie cutter, ca. 1930-50. 2" h. x 2.5" w. $8-10.

Silverplated prize cup, engraved "Boston Terrier Club / Special Prize Cup" on one side, and "Mineola 1896 / For the Best Brace / Won By / Squanto and His Nibs / Owned By / W. G. Kendall." Reed and Barton (Massachusetts), ca. 1896. 4.5" h. x 6" w. $95-125.

Silverplated prize cup, engraved "1st Prize / French Bull Dog or Bitch / Haverhill Kennel Club / 3-22-02 / by T.H. Cornish." Tufts (Massachusetts), ca. 1902. 5.5" h. x 6" w. $95-125.

Sterling silver prize pieces. (Left) Cup, engraved "T.V.K.C. [Tonawanda Valley, N.Y. Kennel Club] / 1941 / Irish Wolfhound," ca. 1941. 2.5" h. x 2" diam. $40-50. (Right) Small tray, engraved "G.V.K.C. [Genesee Valley, N.Y. Kennel Club] / 1941 / Best of Breed," ca. 1941. 3.5" h. x 4" w. $40-50.

(Left) Silverplated medallion, "Collie Club of America / Awarded to [blank]," shepherd's crook and foliage motif, ca. 1886-1900. 2.5" diam. $195-225. (Right) Sterling silver medallion, "Brunswick Foxhound Club /1888," head of Foxhound, marked on reverse "N.G. Wood & Sons, Boston" [Massachusetts], ca. 1910. 1.5" diam. $200-250.

(Top left) Silverplated prize medallion, "Farmers and Mechanics Association, Attleborough, Mass.," with engraved dog's head; engraved on reverse: "Awarded to Pike and Fuller / Champion Prize / for / Fox Hound 'Captain' / Sept. 15, 1885." 1.75" diam. $225-250. (Right) Silvertoned metal prize medal, "Lynn [Massachusetts] Kennel Club / Org. 1904," with head of spaniel; engraved on reverse: "F.B.D.C. of N.E. [French Bull Dog Club of New England] / Boston, 1908 / Won by / Mdlle. Babbette." $85-95. (Lower left) Copper prize medal, "Ladies Kennel Association of Massachusetts," seal of Massachusetts with three dogs' heads; engraved on reverse: "Won by / Brockton Ino / Braintree / 1904." 1.25" diam. $85-95.

Hand-painted copper stamp holder, head of Pointer, ca. 1920-40. 1" h. x 1.75" diam. $65-75.

Lithographed tin tip tray, Pointer in field, "Young Rip Rap," ca. 1900-10. 3.25" h. x 5" w. $75-95.

Lithographed tin "Mascot" safe bank, Chein Manufacturing Company, New Jersey, ca. 1914. Smooth-coated Fox Terrier. 4" h. x 3" w. x 2.5" d. $60-75.

European snuff tins picturing Papillon, four of the same shown from different sides, ca. 1930-50. 2" h. x 1.75 diam. $35-45 each.

English toffee tin, Afghan Hounds, ca. 1950. 1.25" h. x 5" w. x 3.75" d. $10-15.

Round metal beer tray, "Hanley's Peerless Ale," English Bulldog, James Hanley Company [brewery], Providence, Rhode Island, manufactured by American Art Works, Coshocton, Ohio, ca. 1940-50. 12" diam. See the Morgan Dennis oil painting of the Hanley Brewery bulldog, page 21. $75-95.

# Chapter 4
# PHOTOGRAPHY AND PAPER

## PHOTOGRAPHY

Tintype of three boys and dog, second half nineteenth century. 4" h. x 2.5" w. $30-40.

Sepia carte de visite photograph of three boys and sleeping spaniel, Brattström studio, Eskilstuna, Sweden, late nineteenth century. 4" h. x 2.5" w. $30-40.

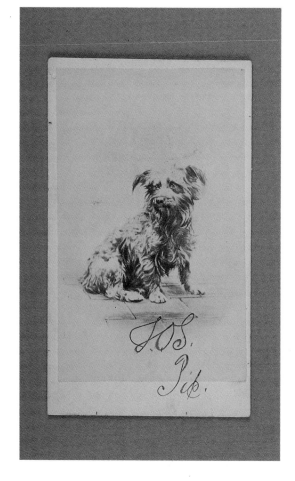

Sepia carte de visite photograph of terrier, Black studio (Boston, Massachusetts), ca. 1860-80. 4" h. x 2.5" w. This little dog's name was Pip; the three handwritten initials above may be "Y.O.S." for "Your Obedient Servant." The "carte de visite" was a mounted photograph measuring 4" x 2.5". Often abbreviated as "CDVs," such photographs were used as calling cards when paying visits, hence the French term. $45-65.

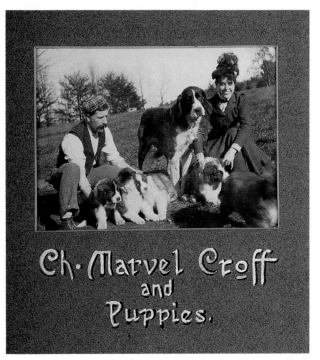

Two of the individual photographs from the St. Bernard grouping on previous page.

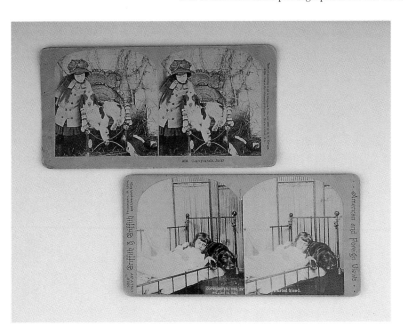

(Top) Sepia-toned stereocard, girl with dog in rustic outdoor chair, ca. 1882. 3.5" h. x 7" w. $7-10. (Bottom) Sepia-toned stereocard, dog at children's bed, ca. 1898. 3.5" h. x 7" w. $7-10.

Two color stereocards, ca. 1905-15. (Top) "Now, Children, You Must Kiss and Make Up." (Bottom) "Trying to Be Good." Each 3.5" h. x 7" w. $7-10 each.

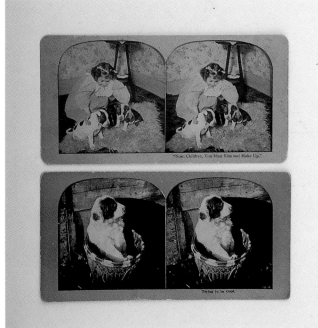

Color stereocard of puppies in basket, "The Kindergarten Class," Chicago, The World View Co., ca. 1910. 3.5" h. x 7" w. $7-10.

Photographic "bookmark" postcard, "Dog Train, North West," ca. 1920-40. 1.75" h. x 5.5" w. $5-7.

Pair of color stereocards, ca. 1905-15. (Top) Boy and English Setter, "The Hunters Talking Over the Day's Sport." (Bottom) "The Hunter's Reverie." Each 3.5" h. x 7" w. $15-25/pair

Photograph of Husky, written on back: "Bertha with the blue eyes .... the wolves got her." Ca. 1930-50. 3.5" h. x 4.75" w. $8-12.

Studio photograph of dog sitting up, unidentified, ca. 1890-1915. 5.25" h. x 2.75" w. $20-30.

Enlarged and highlighted photograph of
Pomeranian from Provanna Kennels,
Rowley, Massachusetts, ca. 1935. 29" h.
x 15.5" w. $75-95.

Color postcard, "Types of English Beauty," English Bulldogs, "Animal Studies" Series, Raphael Tuck & Sons, England, ca. 1900-10. 3.5" h. x 5.5" w. $7-10.

Color postcard, "Spaniel & Retriever," "Animal Life" Series, Raphael Tuck & Sons, England, ca. 1900-10. 3.5" h. x 5.5" w. $7-10.

Color postcard, "Old Towser, " bulldog, ca. 1910, 3.5" h x 5.5" w. This image was adapted from Sir Edwin Landseer's painting *Low Life*. A trade card inspired by his companion painting, *High Life*, is pictured on page 88. $7-10.

Color postcard, Pekingese puppies, artist-signed P. Kirmse, "Little Sweethearts" Series, Raphael Tuck & Sons, England, ca. 1920-30. Persis Kirmse (1884-1955), an accomplished animal artist in her own right, was the sister of Marguerite Kirmse—a name more well-known in the United States since Marguerite moved to the U.S. from England in 1917 and remained until her death in 1954. 3.5" h. x 5.5" w. $7-10.

Tinted postcard, "Toy French Poodle," ca. 1910. 3.5" h. x 5.5" w. $5-7.

Black and white postcard, "Red Irish Setter," ca. 1904. 3.5" h. x 5.5" w. $5-7.

Color postcards, artist-signed Birst, (left) Schnauzer, (right) Boxer, ca. 1950. Each 3.5" h. x 5.5" w. $5-7 each.

Color postcard, "Making a Fool of Him," Bloodhound at dinner table, ca. 1905-10. 3.5" h. x 5.5" w. $5-7.

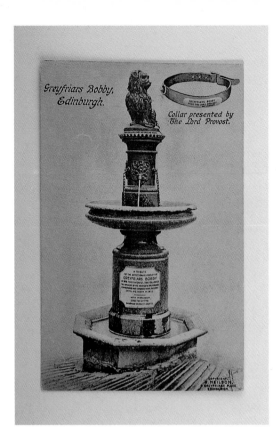

Black and white postcard, Greyfriars Bobby [Skye Terrier] monument, Edinburgh, Scotland, ca. 1920-40. 3.5" h. x 5.5" w. $5-7.

Two black and white postcards picturing dog families, ca. 1905-15. Each 3.5" h. x 5.5" w. $5-7 each.

Two black and white postcards of Linn's Famous Educated Dogs, ca. 1900-20. Each 3.5" h. x 5.5" w. $7-10 each.

Black and white postcard, "Where's That Boatman?" Eleven terriers in boat, England, ca. 1915. 3.5" x 5.5". $7-10.

Tinted postcard, "A Dog Cart," Québec, Canada, ca. 1910-30. 3.5" h. x 5.5" w. $5-7.

Two tinted postcards, hunt clubs in (top) Medford, Massachusetts and (bottom) Pinehurst, North Carolina, ca. 1915-30. Each 3.5" h. x 5.5" w. $5-7 each.

Color postcard, Irish Setter puppies in hunting pouch, ca. 1910. 3.5" h. x 5.5" w. $5-7.

Tinted postcard, "The Campman and Dog," ca. 1905-10. 3.5" h. x 5.5" w. $7-10.

Color postcard, dog resembling Vizsla, Europe, ca. 1905-15. 3.5" h. x 5.5" w. $5-7.

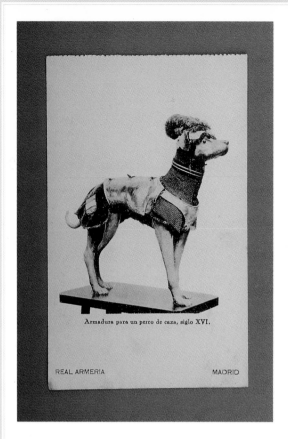

Armadura para un perro de caza, siglo XVI.

REAL ARMERIA          MADRID

Black and white postcard, sixteenth-century dog armor, Spain, ca. 1920-40. 3.5" h. x 5.5" w. $7-10.

Black and white World War I postcard, "Some Patriot," Alsatian or German Shepherd Dog, ca. 1914-18. 3.5" h. x 5.5" w. $10-15.

Color World War II postcard, "Let's Grin and Wear It, Folks!" West Highland White Terrier, England, ca. 1940-45. 3.5" h. x 5.5" w. $7-10.

"LET'S GRIN AND WEAR IT, FOLKS!"

World War I postcards. (Left) Sepia-toned, "Tommy and His Mascot," England. (Center) Color, "Has Anyone Seen a German Band?" England. (Right) Black and white, "The Aisne Front. French Grenadier and His Sentinel Dog," France. All ca. 1914-1918. $10-15 each.

Chromolithograph album card, "Preparing for a Journey," sled dogs, ca. 1882. 2.75" h. x 4.25" w. $5-8.

Two chromolithograph calling cards, Greyhounds, ca. 1870-90. Each 1.25" h. x 2.5" w. $5-7 each.

Left: Chromolithograph round album card with attached silk fringe, girl with puppies, ca. 1870-90. 4" diam. $8-10.

Below: Chromolithograph tambourine-shaped album card, boy and terrier, ca. 1880. 3" diam. $8-10.

Chromolithograph album card, "Japanese Spaniel" (Japanese Chin), ca. 1900. 5" h. x 3.5" w. $8-10.

Left: Chromolithograph Reward of Merit card (shown front and back), Maltese, Smooth-coated Fox Terrier, and Pekingese (or Pug?), ca. 1885. 5.5" h. x 3.5" w. $8-10.

Group of Victorian
chromolithograph
die-cut "scraps," used
for decorating album
pages and home-
made objects, ca.
1870-90. Various
sizes. $5-15 each.

Cigarette card album, *An Album of Dogs*, Cairn Terrier on cover, issued by W.D. & H.O. Wills (Great Britain), ca. 1937. Contains complete set of fifty color cigarette cards. 5" h. x 7.25" w. $200-225. Shown with assorted loose Wills dog breed cigarette cards. Each 1.5" h. x 2.75" w. $4-6 each. Cigarette cards originated in the late nineteenth century as printed cardboard stiffeners for paper packages of cigarettes. Later, they came to be issued as pictorial cards that could be collected in sets and displayed in special albums. The dog-themed cards shown in this chapter were produced by British firms between the two world wars.

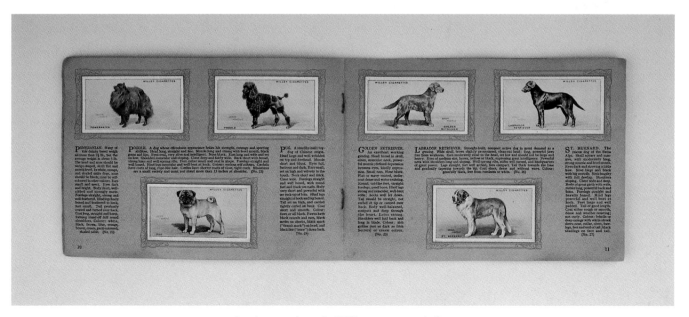

Inside pages from the Wills cigarette card album.

Group of color cigarette cards, Gallaher's, London and Belfast, ca. 1935. Each approx. 2.5" h. x 3" w. $4-6 each.

Group of color cigarette cards after paintings by Arthur Wardle, John Player & Sons, Branch of Imperial Tobacco Company (of Great Britain & Ireland), Ltd., ca. 1935. Each approx. 3" h. x 2.5" w. $4-6 each.

Group of black and white cigarette cards, "Dogs & Friend " Series, "described by Lady Kitty Ritson" (a prominent dog fancier of the day), Carreras Ltd., London, ca. 1936. Each approx. 2.5" h. x 1.25" w. $4-6 each.

Group of black and white cigarette cards, Senior Service, England, ca. 1939. Each approx. 2" h. x 3" w. $4-6 each.

Group of cigarette cards, Imperial Tobacco Company of Canada, Ltd., ca. 1935. Each approx. 1.5" h. x 2.5" w. $4-6 each.

Close-up of "Curly Retriever" Imperial Tobacco Company cigarette card, with information on back of card.

Christmas cards picturing dogs. (Top left) Color postcard, three unclipped Poodles or Havanese dogs, ca. 1905. 3.5" h. x 5.5" w. $5-7. (Top right) Color postcard, dog pulling skater, ca. 1905. 3.5" h. x 5.5" w. $5-7. (Lower left) Greeting card with Scottish Terrier, ca. 1940. 3" h. x 4" w. $5-7. (Lower right) Album card, ca. 1880-90. 3.25" h. x 2.25" w. $5-7.

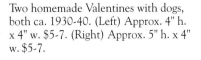

Two homemade Valentines with dogs, both ca. 1930-40. (Left) Approx. 4" h. x 4" w. $5-7. (Right) Approx. 5" h. x 4" w. $5-7.

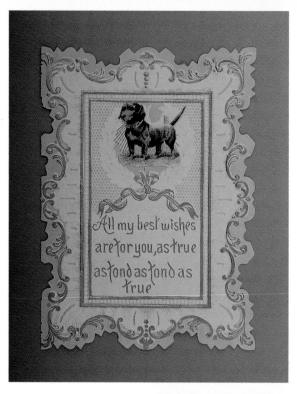

Greeting card with Dachshund, ca. 1915-30. 5" h. x 3.75" w. $7-10.

Receipt form with dog's head, ca. 1906. 3" h. x 8.75" w. $10-15.

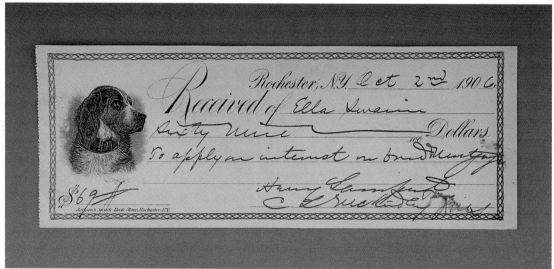

Blank promissory note form with dog's head, ca. 1890-1910. 3.25" h. x 8.25" w. $10-15.

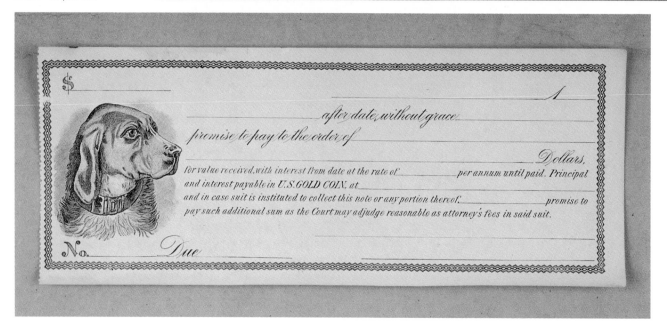

Right:
City of Boston (Massachusetts) dog license document for a black Newfoundland named Gip, 1893. 10.25" h. x 8.5" w. $40-50.

Bottom left:
Calendar sample, color illustration of woman and dog with flower basket, ca. 1936. 7.75" h. x 5.75" w. $25-35.

Bottom right:
Cardboard penny bank, German Shepherd Dog, distributed by John Hancock Mutual Life Insurance Company, Boston, Massachusetts, ca. 1930-50. 6" h. x 4.5" w. $15-25.

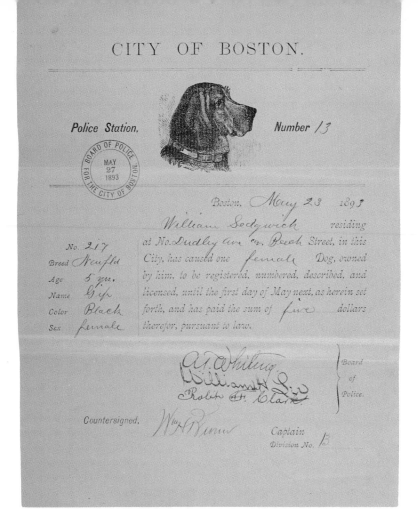

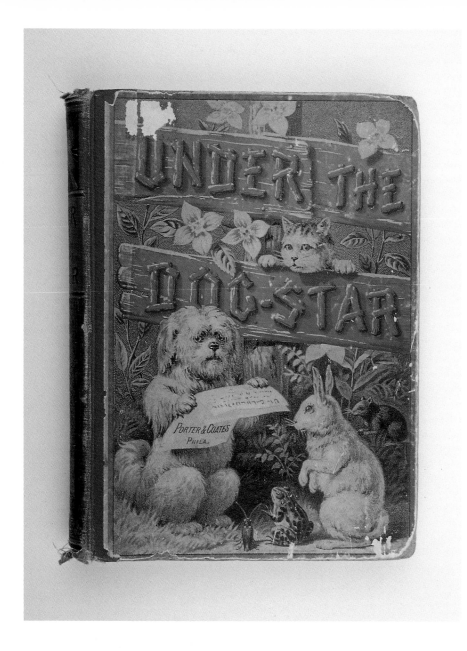

Children's book, *Under the Dog-Star: From the Dog-Latin of Jock*, by Margaret Vandegrift, Philadelphia, Pennsylvania, Porter & Coates, 1881. Chromolithograph on board covers. 8.75" h. x 6.5" w. Jock is a Skye Terrier. $45-65.

Frontispiece and title page from *Under the Dog-Star.*

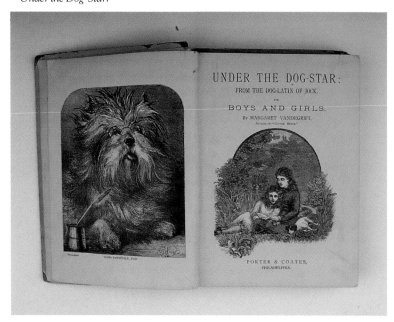

Chapter entitled "Dash Does Errands" from children's book *Dog Stories*, compiled by Asa Bullard, Boston, Massachusetts, Lee & Shepard, 1863. Embossed cloth over boards. 4.5" h. x 3" w. $35-45.

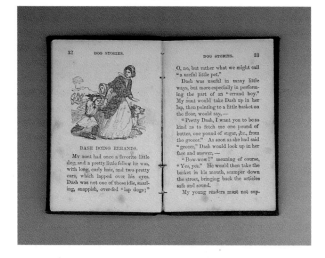

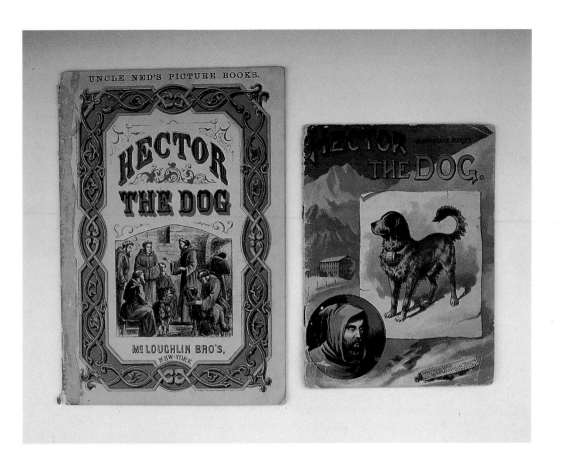

Two editions of the children's book *Hector the Dog*, both New York, McLoughlin Bros., both bound in paper covers. (Left) Ca. 1880. 10.5" h. x 7.25" w. $30-40. (Right) Ca. 1889. 8" h. x 6.25" w. $25-35.

Illustration from *Old Mother Hubbard.*

Left:

Children's book, *Old Mother Hubbard and her Dog*, New York, McLoughlin Bros., ca. 1889. Chromolithograph paper covers. The dog pictured here, although closely resembling the modern-day Samoyed or Eskimo Dog, is probably the old White Pomeranian breed. Larger than the Pomeranian we recognize today, this dog was prominent in the past. See the pair of bisque figures on page 40, the chalkware dog in the photograph on page 71, and the little painted plaster figure on page 138. 11" h. x 9" w. $40-45.

Children's book, *Dash's Holiday*, New York, McLoughlin Bros., ca. 1880. Chromolithograph paper covers. "Dash" was one of the most popular dog names of the late nineteenth century, perhaps because it was the name of Queen Victoria's favorite spaniel. 10.25" h. x 7.25" w. $35-45.

Illustrations from *Dash's Holiday*.

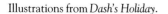

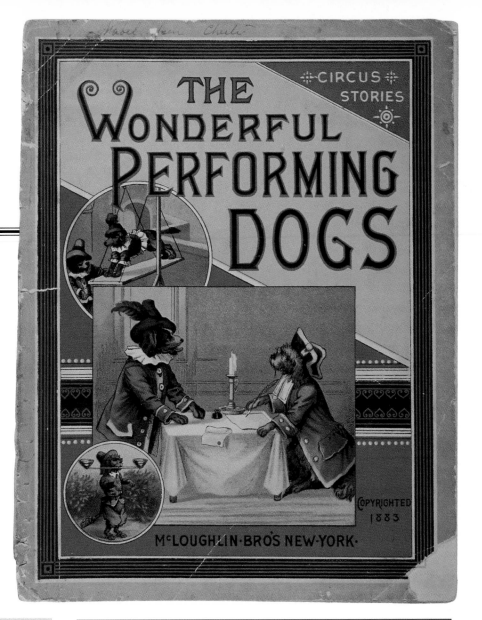

Children's book, *The Wonderful Performing Dogs*, New York, McLoughlin Bros., 1883. Color paper covers. 10.5" h. x 8.25" w. $35-45.

Children's book, *The Dog That Rang the Bell*, D.C. Cook Publishing Company, 1914. Color paper covers. 6" h. x 4" w. $10-15.

Children's book, *The Story of Rin-Tin-Tin, the Marvelous and Amazing Dog of the Movies*, Racine, Wisconsin, Whitman Publishing Company, 1927. Color paper over board covers. German Shepherd Dog. 9" h. x 6.5" w. $30-40.

Frontispiece spread of book, *The Story of Rin-Tin-Tin.*

Inside back cover illustrations from *The Story of Rin-Tin-Tin.*

Children's book, *Dogs in Rhyme*, International Paper Goods Company, 1927. Color paper covers.
Boston Terrier puppies. 14.25" h. x 8.5" w. $20-25.

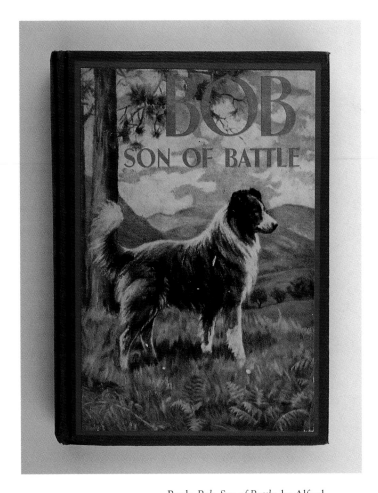

Book, *Igloo*, by Jane Brevoort Walden, with Foreword by Richard E. Byrd, Rear Admiral, U.S.N., Ret. Illustrations by Diana Thorne, New York, G.P. Putnam's Sons, 1931. Autographed by the author, original dust jacket, cloth binding. Igloo was the Smooth-coated Fox Terrier who accompanied Admiral Byrd on his polar expeditions. 9" h. x 6.6" w. $50-65.

Book, *Bob, Son of Battle*, by Alfred Ollivant, illustrations by Marguerite Kirmse, New York, Garden City Publishing Company, 1935. Cloth binding with color illustration. Collie-type dog. 9" h. x 6.5" w. $30-40.

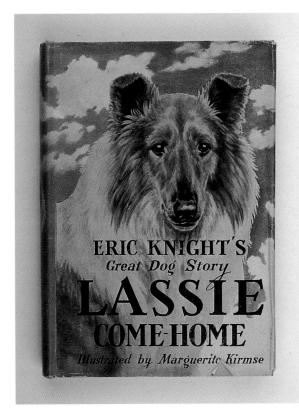

Book, *Lassie Come-Home*, by Eric Knight, illustrations by Marguerite Kirmse, Philadelphia, Pennsylvania, John C. Winston Company, 1944. Original dust jacket, cloth binding. Collie. 8.75" h. x 6" w. $30-40.

Ch. Blackmoor Barnabas of Giralda
A.K.C. A 248532

Giralda Farms                    Madison, N. J.

Color frontispiece plate, "Ch. Blackmoor Barnabas of Giralda, A.K.C. A248532, Giralda Farms, Madison, N.J.," from *The English Cocker Spaniel in America*, by Geraldine R. Dodge, New York, The English Cocker Spaniel Club of America, 1942. Cloth binding. 19" h. x 7.5" w. Book: $150-200.

Book, *Training the Rabbit Hound: A Book on Bassets and Beagles*, by Carl E. Smith, rev. 5th ed., Chicago, Illinois, Wilcox & Follett Co., 1944. Cloth binding. 7.75" h. x 5.25" w. $25-35.

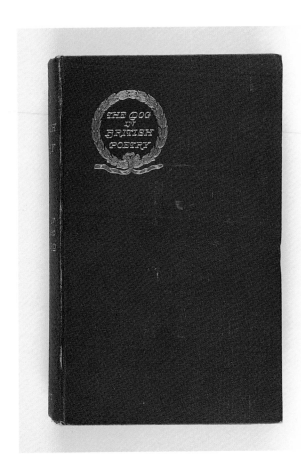

Book, *The Dog in British Poetry*, London, David Nutt, 1893. Blue cloth binding, 7.75" h. x 5" w. $40-50.

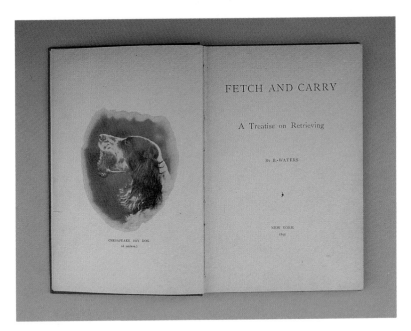

Frontispiece and title page of *Fetch and Carry: A Treatise on Retrieving*, by B. Waters, New York, Forest and Stream Publishing Company, 1895. Cloth binding. Note that the frontispiece of an English Setter is misidentified as a Chesapeake Bay Dog. 7.5" h. x 5" w. $50-65.

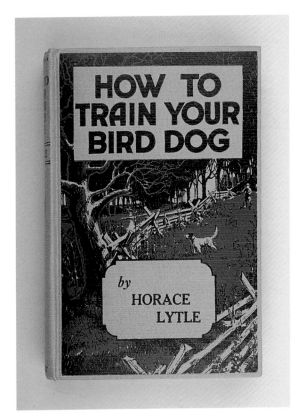

Book, *How To Train Your Bird Dog*, by Horace Lytle, Dayton, Ohio, A.F. Hochwalt Company, 1946. Printed cloth binding. 7.5" h. x 5" w. $25-35.

Pamphlet, *Your Dog,* Potter & Wrightington, Boston, Massachusetts, ca. 1910. West Highland White Terriers. 6" h. x 3.75" w. $10-15.

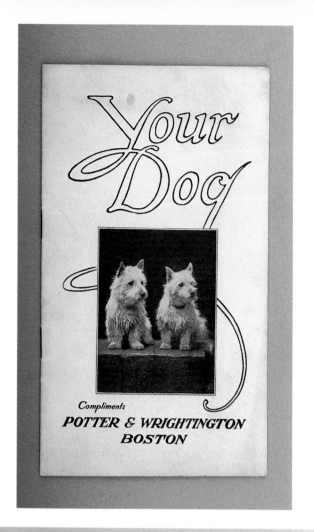

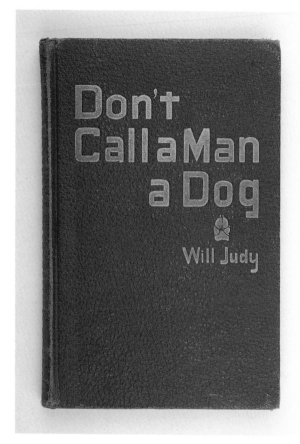

Book, *Don't Call a Man A Dog,* by Will Judy, Chicago, Illinois, Judy Publishing Company, 1949. Cloth binding. 8.5" h. x 5.75" w. $25-35.

Book, *Surfman: The Adventures of a Coast Guard Dog,* by Col. S.P. Meek, New York, Knopf, 1950. Autographed by author, original dust jacket, cloth binding. Chesapeake Bay Retriever. $35-45.

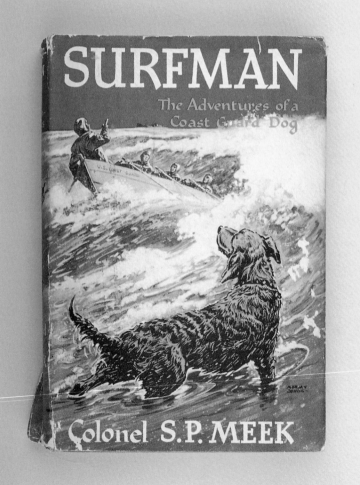

Pamphlet, *Spratt's Hints on the Care and Feeding of Dogs*, 1936. Spaniels. 7.5" h. x 5.25" w. $10-15.

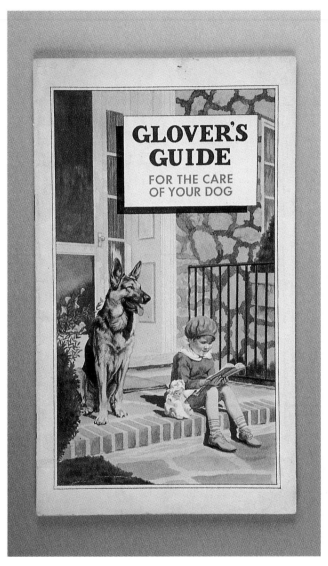

Pamphlet, *Glover's Guide for the Care of Your Dog*, 1934. German Shepherd Dog. 8" h. x 4.75" w. $10-15.

Pamphlet, *Dogs, Care and Feeding*, Wirthmore Dog Food Company, Boston, Massachusetts, 1947. Husky. 9" h. x 6" w. $10-15.

Magazine cover, *Pictorial Review*, May 1923, illustration of Pekingese in woman's hands by Tadé Styka. 16" h. x 10.5" w. $10-15.

BELGIAN SCHIPPERKE

Color illustration of Belgian Schipperke removed from *The Book of Dogs*, By Louis Agassiz Fuertes and others, Washington, D.C., National Geographic Society, 1919. 3.75" h. x 5.5" w. $7-10.

CHIHUAHUA          MEXICAN HAIRLESS

Chihuahua and Mexican Hairless, also from *The Book of Dogs*.

CURLY POODLE     TOY POODLE     CORDED POODLE

Curly Poodle, Toy Poodle, Corded Poodle, also from *The Book of Dogs*.

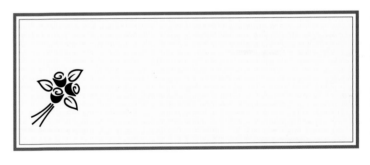

DACHSHUND

Dachshund, also from *The Book of Dogs*.

# Chapter 5
# WOOD

## FIGURES

Small hand-carved wooden Boxer or Boston Terrier figure, painted detail, probably Germany, ca. 1930-50. 1.75" h. x 1.75" w. $35-45.

Small, hand-carved wooden recumbent St. Bernard figure, painted detail, probably Germany, early twentieth century. 1" h. x 3.5" w. $65-75.

Small, hand-carved wooden Doberman Pinscher figure, painted detail, probably Germany, ca. 1930-50. 2" h. x 2.5" w. $35-45.

Small, hand-carved wooden Great Dane figure, painted detail, probably Germany, ca. 1930-50. 3.25" h. x 3.5" w. $35-45.

Hand-carved wooden howling puppy figure, painted detail, probably Germany, ca. 1930-50. 4.5" h. x 5" w. Tail repair. $75-85.

Hand-carved wooden St. Bernard figure, painted detail, probably Germany, ca. 1930-50. 3.25" h. x 5" w. $65-75.

# OTHER WOODEN ITEMS

Hand-carved wooden crop or cane top, two dogs' heads, early twentieth century. 2" h. x 2.5" w. $85-100.

Hand-carved wooden dog's head cane top, glass eyes, Germany, early twentieth century. 4" h. x 2" w. $85-100.

Small painted silhouette of woman and Irish Setter on wooden plaque, label on back: "From the Workshop of A.B. Pond, 75 Quincy Street, Medford, Mass." Ca. 1920-35. 4.5" h. x 3" w. $35-45.

Hand-carved wooden dog's head bottle stopper, glass eyes, Germany, ca. 1950. 4" h. x 1.75" w. $65-85.

Hand-carved wooden Airedale head corkscrew and bottle stopper, probably Germany, ca. 1930-50. Each 4" h. x 2" w. $65-85 each.

Round woodburnt plaque, puppy in muzzle, "All I Did Was Growl a Little," Flemish Art, dated 1908 on back. Woodburning, or pyrography, was a popular pastime early in the twentieth century, and "Flemish Art" craft patterns were widely available. 5.5" diam. $35-45.

Round woodburnt plaque, head of Foxhound, Flemish Art, ca. 1905-1915. 5.75" diam. $35-45.

Oval woodburnt plaque, two puppies under umbrella, Flemish Art, ca. 1905-15. 13.5" w. $65-85.

Wooden lattice comb case or wall pocket, incised dog motif, late nineteenth century. 14" h. x 12" w. $85-100.

Cutout wooden hanging corner shelf, two sitting retrievers, made in Waterville, Maine, ca. 1950. 18" h. x 9.5" w. $85-100.

Hand-carved wooden tie rack with dog motif, ca. 1940-50. 4.5" h. x 9" w. $45-60.

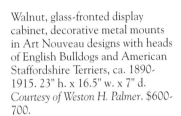

Walnut, glass-fronted display cabinet, decorative metal mounts in Art Nouveau designs with heads of English Bulldogs and American Staffordshire Terriers, ca. 1890-1915. 23" h. x 16.5" w. x 7" d. *Courtesy of Weston H. Palmer.* $600-700.

Detail, showing American Staffordshire Terrier head mount. (See similar piece on candy box, page 142.)

Detail, showing English Bulldog head mount.

Cherry cigarette box, metal lining, with sitting terrier figure on lid, label inside: "Yawman and Erbe Mfg. Co., Rochester, New York," ca. 1930-50. 2.5" h. x 7.5" w. x 3.5" d. $65-85.

Pair of painted wooden stylized Scottish Terrier bookends, ca. 1930-50. 5" h. x 5" w. $35-45/pair.

Hand-carved wooden sculpture of head of Irish Setter mounted as lamp base, ca. 1950. 24" h. x 8.75" w. $125-150.

Stencilled rug pattern on burlap, dog with slipper design, H.B. Bennett & Co., Portland, Maine, late nineteenth-early twentieth century. H.B. Bennett was listed in the 1879 Portland, Maine City Directory as "stencil cutter," but by 1900 was president of his own firm. 26" h. x 49" w. $100-150.

Oval hand-hooked rug, wool on burlap, grey dog with floral and landscape motif, initials "S.M.", linen backing, ca. 1920-40. Some losses, wear. 21" h. x 53" w. $600-800.

Rectangular hand-hooked rug, recumbent tan dog motif, wool and cotton on burlap, ca. 1920-40. Repaired, rebound. 29.5" h. x 53" w. $350-450.

Rectangular hand-hooked Scottish Terrier rug, wool and cotton on burlap, ca. 1930-50. Rebacked. 21.5" h. x 36" w. $350-400.

Cotton filet crochet piece, two puppies and cow, early twentieth century. 18" h. x 16" w. $30-40.

Cotton damask tea towel with filet crochet inset, dog motif, early twentieth century. 21" h. x 12.5" w. $15-20.

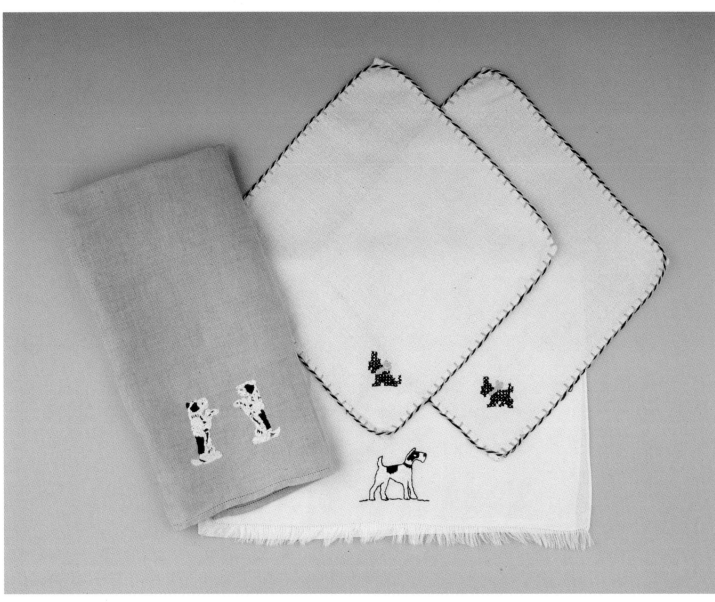

Embroidered linens. (Left) Blue linen tea towel with begging Wire-haired Fox Terriers, ca. 1920-40. 29" h. x 13.5" w. $8-15. (Right) Two linen napkins with Scottish Terriers, ca. 1930-50. Each 8" sq. $5-8 each. (Bottom) White linen tea towel with Wire-haired Fox Terrier, ca. 1920-40. 16" h. x 11.5" w. $8-15.

Left:
Celluloid pendant on black silk ribbon, silhouette of lady taking Greyhound's paw, ca. 1930s. Pendant: 2" h. x 1.5" w. Ribbon: 18". $75-100.

Right:
Silvertoned metal openwork brooch, Schnauzer and bird motif, ca. 1940-50. 2" h. x 1.5" w. $45-60.

Silvertoned metal racing Greyhound pin, ca. 1930-50. 1.75" long. $20-30.

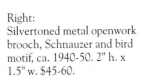

Enameled terrier pins, ca. 1930-50. Each approx. 1.5" h. x 1.5" w. $45-65 each.

Wooden brooch in shape of three diamonds, figures of terrier and English Bulldog flanking initial "C", early twentieth century. 1.25" h. x 3" w. $65-75.

Sterling silver brooch, two stylized Greyhounds or Borzoi, ca. 1930-50. 1.75" h. x 2" w. $85-100.

Three sterling silver pins, each ca. 1950. (Top) Pointer, Mexico. 1.25" h. x 2" w. $65-85. (Lower left) French Bulldog. 1.5" h. x 2" w. $65-85. (Lower right) Boxer. 1" h. x 1" w. $50-65.

Two Bakelite pins. (Left) Reverse crystal of Wire-haired Fox Terrier mounted on two Bakelite discs, ca. 1930-40. 1.25" diam. $50-75. (Right) Spaniel head on Bakelite oval, ca. 1930-40. 1.5" long. $45-60.

(Left) Silvertoned metal Doberman Pinscher pin, c. 1950. (Right) Silvertoned metal German Shepherd pin, c. 1950. Each approx. 1.5". $15-25 each.

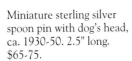

Wood and brass brooch, three terrier heads, ca. 1930-50. 2.25" long. $65-75.

Miniature sterling silver spoon pin with dog's head, ca. 1930-50. 2.5" long. $65-75.

Silvertoned metal charm bracelet, Poodle, Scottish Terrier, and Maltese head charms, ca. 1950. 6.5" long. $35-45.

# Chapter 8
# MISCELLANEOUS

Hand-carved marble figure of recumbent Mastiff, glass eyes, late nineteenth century. 3.5" h. x 6.25" w. $150-200.

Small painted plaster sitting dog, White Pomeranian type, ca. 1920-40. 2.25" h. x 2" w. $25-35.

Small hard rubber Collie figure, early twentieth century. 1.75" h. x 3" w. $35-45.

Small painted plaster dog figure, probably from crèche set, Italy, ca. 1930-50. 2.75" h. x 2.25" w. $20-30.

Small celluloid dog figure, Landseer Newfoundland, ca. 1920-40. 1.5" h. x 2.5" w. $35-45.

Painted plaster figural desk or pin tray, recumbent dog with cat, early twentieth century. 4.5" h. x 7" w. $65-75.

Victorian stone-like figural group, seated girl with large dog and terrier, ca. 1870-90. 14" h. x 7" w. $275-325.

Painted composition sitting English
Bulldog figure, glass eyes, ca. 1920-50.
7" h. x 7" w. Tail abrasion. $65-85.

Painted composition spaniel pull toy with moving feet, ca. 1920-40. 7" h. x 11" w. $150-225.

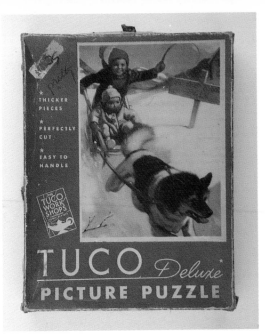

Tuco Deluxe Picture Puzzle, boxed cardboard jigsaw puzzle picturing Husky pulling two children on sled, ca. 1940-50. Completed puzzle, 19.25" h. x 15" w. $35-45.

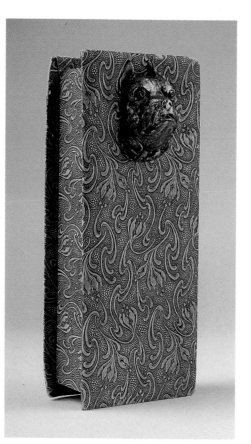

Pasteboard candy box covered with Art Nouveau-motif embossed paper, attached three-dimensional white metal mount of head of American Staffordshire Terrier (see similar mount on walnut cabinet, page 123.) Russell's Chocolates, Cambridge, Massachusetts, ca. 1890-1915. 1.5" h. x 3" w. x 7" long (shown standing on end). $65-75.

Pasteboard candy box with ribbon, two postcards of Wire-haired Fox Terrier puppies on lid. Pencil inscription inside dated 1943. 1.25" h. x 4.5" w. x 13.25" long. $25-35.

Red plush writing box, with copper-finished bas-relief panels, top panel of hunting dogs scene, blue silk interior, patent date 1885. 3.5" h. x 11.5" w. x 8.5" d. $225-275.

Detail, showing top of writing box.

144 🌼

Opposite page, top:
Leather pocket book with beadwork on punched paper, Prince Charles Spaniel motif (some losses). Brass fittings, interior compartments for calling cards, notepad, and pencil, ca. 1850-80. 3.25" h. x 5.5" w. $225-275.

Opposite page, bottom:
Hand-colored lithograph paper fan on wooden sticks, reclining lady (possibly a depiction of the actress Sarah Bernhardt, 1844-1923) with recumbent dog—Greyhound or Borzoi? Ca. 1880-1910. 11" h. x 21" w. $65-85.

Hand-painted wooden fan, head of Blenheim Spaniel, thin silk ribbon edging (some breaks), ca. 1880-1910. 5.5" h. x 9" w. $125-175.

Paper advertising fan on wooden stick, St. Bernard's head, celebrating the Centennial of Orange, Massachusetts, 1910. 14" h. x 8" w. $45-65.

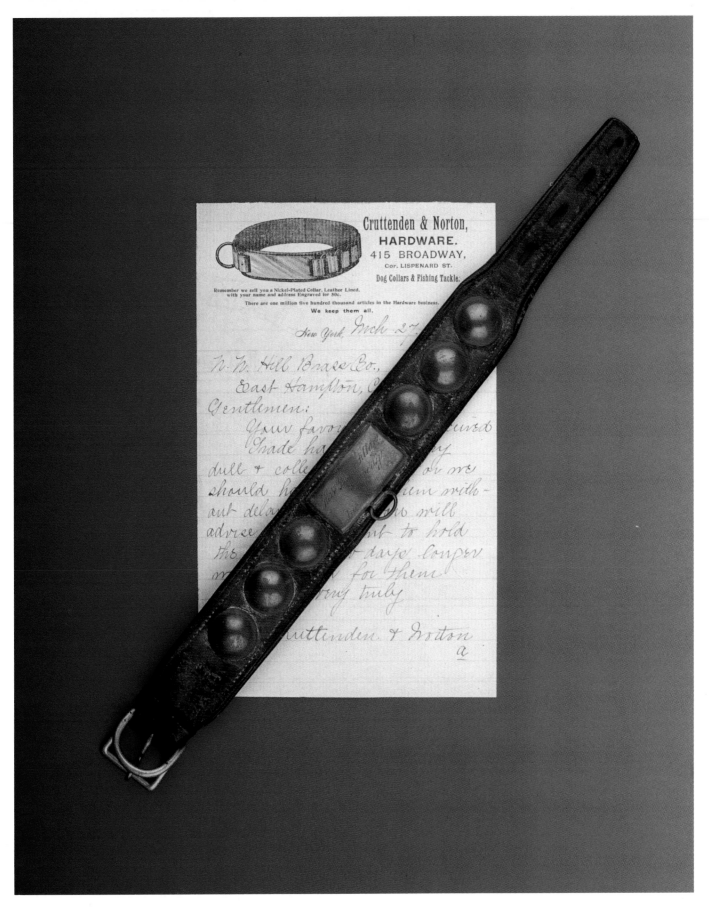

Heavy leather and brass dog collar, engraved on nameplate: "Mrs. Bryce Allan, Beverly / Lic. [blank]" Ca. 1890-1915. 15.5" l. x 1.5" w. $195-225. Shown with the letterhead of Cruttenden & Norton Hardware [New York City]—"Dog Collars and Fishing Tackle," ca. 1896. 9.25" h. x 6" w. $20-30.

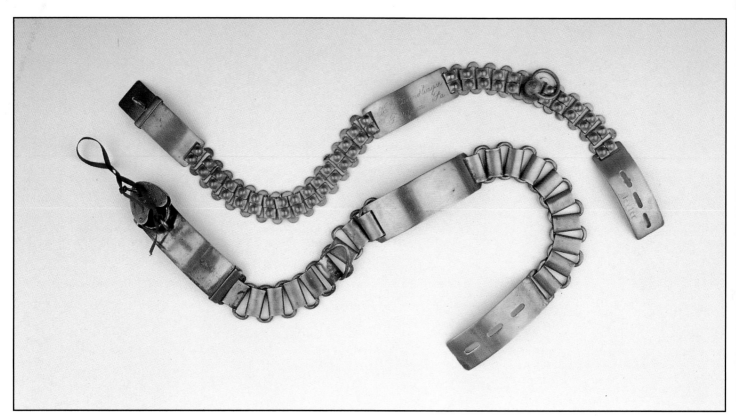

(Top) Brass linked dog collar, engraved on nameplate: "H Y Brendlinger / Pottstown Pa," also engraved on clasp with dog's name "Dexter." Ca. 1890-1915. 18.5" l. x 1" w. $275-325.

(Bottom) Brass-plated linked dog collar with original lock and key, "N.W. & Co." on lock, collar nameplate blank, ca. 1890-1915. $275-325.

Steel link over leather dog collar, nameplate engraved: "R.B. Wellman / Thurlow Pa" Locked with small padlock, key missing. Early twentieth century. 22" l. x 1.25" w. $250-300.

Detail of pin-back buttons.

Group of metal pin-back buttons, various dog breeds, ca. 1930-50. Each .75" diam. $10-15 each.

Three dog show prize ribbons, 1938-1940. Each 8" h. x 2.75" w. $5-10 each.

Small penknife with Dachshund motif,
ca. 1940-50. 2.25" long. $10-15.

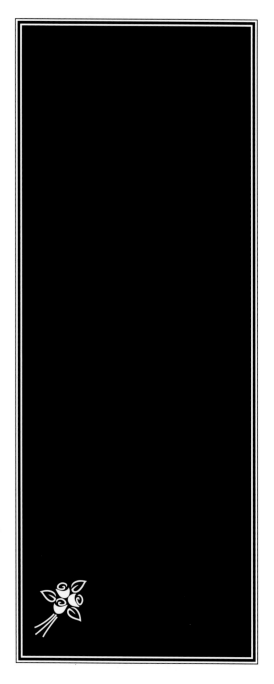

Unopened box of "Bull Dog" brand
canning jar rubbers, ca. 1945. 3.5" h. x
3.5" w. x 1.5" d. $25-35.

# BIBLIOGRAPHY

## BOOKS

American Kennel Club. *The Complete Dog Book*, 16th ed. New York: Howell Book House, 1983.

Bishop, Robert. *The All-American Dog: Man's Best Friend in Folk Art*. New York: Avon, 1977.

Bonhams [Auction House]. *Dogs and Cats in Art* [auction catalog], London, January 22, 1997.

Bradley, Elizabeth. *Decorative Victorian Needlework*. New York: Clarkson Potter, 1990.

Clark, Kenneth. *Animals and Men*. New York: Morrow, 1977.

Congdon-Martin, Douglas. *Figurative Cast Iron: A Collector's Guide*. Atglen, Pa.: Schiffer Publishing, Ltd., 1994.

Conti, Achille Alessandro and Ptolemy Tompkins. *A Dog Lover's Collection*. New York: M.T. Train/Scala Books, dist. by Antique Collectors' Club, 1995.

Davis, Candace Sten and Patricia Baugh. *A Treasury of Scottie Dog Collectibles: Identification and Values*. Paducah, Ky.: Collector Books, 1998.

Davis, Henry P., ed. *The Modern Dog Encyclopedia*. 3rd ed. Harrisburg, Pa.: Stackpole, 1958.

DeBolt, C. Gerald. *DeBolt's Dictionary of American Pottery Marks: Whiteware and Porcelain*. Paducah, Ky.: Collector Books, 1994.

Gascoigne, Bamber. *How to Identify Prints*. London: Thames and Hudson, 1986.

Godden, Geoffrey A. *Encyclopaedia of British Pottery and Porcelain Marks*. Exton, Pa.: Schiffer Publishing, Ltd., 1964.

Hausman, Gerald and Loretta Hausman. *The Mythology of Dogs: Canine Legend and Lore Through the Ages*. New York: St. Martin's, 1997.

Heritage Plantation of Sandwich [Massachusetts] *Canines & Felines: Dogs and Cats in American Art* [exhibition catalog], Sandwich, May 8 - October 23, 1988.

Howard, Tom. *The Illustrated Dog*. Edison, N.J.: Chartwell Books, 1994.

Jackson, Frank. *Faithful Friends: Dogs in Life and Literature*. New York: Carroll & Graf, 1997.

Kenny, Adele. *Staffordshire Spaniels*. Atglen, Pa.: Schiffer Publishing, Ltd., 1997.

Kuritzky, Louis. *Collector's Guide to Bookends: Identification and Values*. Paducah, Ky.: Collector Books, 1998.

McBride, Gerald P. *A Collector's Guide to Cast-Metal Bookends*. Atglen, Pa.: Schiffer Publishing, Ltd., 1997.

Méry, Fernand. *The Life, History, and Magic of the Dog*. New York: Grosset & Dunlap, 1970.

Muncaster, Alice L. and Ellen Sawyer. *The Dog Made Me Buy It! A Treasury of Dogs Who Sold Yesterday's Products*. New York: Crown, 1990.

Rice, D.G. *English Porcelain Animals of the 19th Century*. Woodbridge, England: Antique Collectors' Club, 1989.

Ritvo, Harriet. *The Animal Estate: The English and Other Creatures in the Victorian Age*. Cambridge, Mass.: Harvard University Press, 1987.

Rosenblum, Robert. *The Dog in Art from Rococo to Post-Modernism*. New York: Abrams, 1988.

Rowan, Roy and Brooke Janis. *First Dogs: American Presidents and Their Best Friends*. Chapel Hill, N.C. : Algonquin Books of Chapel Hill, 1997.

Secord, William. *Dog Painting, 1840-1940: A Social History of the Dog in Art*. Woodbridge, England: Antique Collectors' Club, 1992.

Silverman, Ruth, ed. *The Dog Observed: Photographs, 1844-1983*. New York: Knopf, 1984.

Suarès, J.C., ed. *Hollywood Dogs*. San Francisco: Collins, 1993.

Thurston, Mary Elizabeth. *The Lost History of the Canine Race*. New York: Avon, 1996.

Watson, James. *The Dog Book*. Garden City, N.Y.: Doubleday, Page & Co., 1912.

Wendt, Lloyd M. *Dogs: A Historical Journey*. New York: Howell Book House, 1996.

Williams, Petra. *Staffordshire Romantic Transfer Patterns: Cup Plates and Early Victorian China*. Jeffersontown, Ky.: Fountain House East, 1978.

Winokur, Jon, comp. *Mondo Canine*. New York: Dutton, 1991.

## PERIODICALS

*Canine Collectibles Quarterly*. "Devoted to the promotion, enjoyment, and collection of dog memorabilia." Puppybiscuit Publications, Jane Swanson, Editor, 10290 Hill Road, Erie, IL 61250.

*Canine Images*. Nancy Ann Thompson, Publisher, 1003 Central Avenue, Fort Dodge, IA 50501.

*Classified K-9*. A buying/selling newsletter published bi-monthly, Gail McDonald, Editor, 766 Willard Street #A10, Quincy, MA 02169.

*Paw Prints*. Quarterly newsletter of the International Society of Animal License Collectors, Inc., Bill Bone, Editor, 928 S.R. 2206, Clinton, KY 42031.

*Sirius*. Newsletter of the American Kennel Club Museum of the Dog, Daphne Gentry, Editor, 1721 S. Mason Rd., St. Louis, MO 63131.

# INDEX